Sparkly Things to make and do

Leonie Pratt

Designed and illustrated by Katrina Fearn,
Non Figg, Josephine Thompson, Stella Baggott
and Katie Mayes

Edited by Fiona Watt

Steps illustrated by Stella Baggott
Photographs by Howard Allman

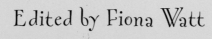

Contents

Sparkly heart strings

1. Place a mug on a piece of pink paper. Draw around it twice and cut out the circles. Then, cut two circles from purple paper, too.

2. Fold all the circles in half. On one circle, draw a half-circle. Then, keeping the paper folded, cut along the line you have drawn.

3. Keeping the small piece folded, draw the shape of half a heart against the fold. Then, carefully cut along the line.

4. Lay the large 'C' shape on a folded circle and draw around the inside. Draw around it again on the other circles. Cut along the lines.

5. Lay the piece with the heart cut out on a folded circle. Draw around the heart and cut it out. Do the same with the other circles.

6. Open out the shapes. Spread glue on a pink ring, then lay a long piece of thread over it. Press a purple ring on top.

2

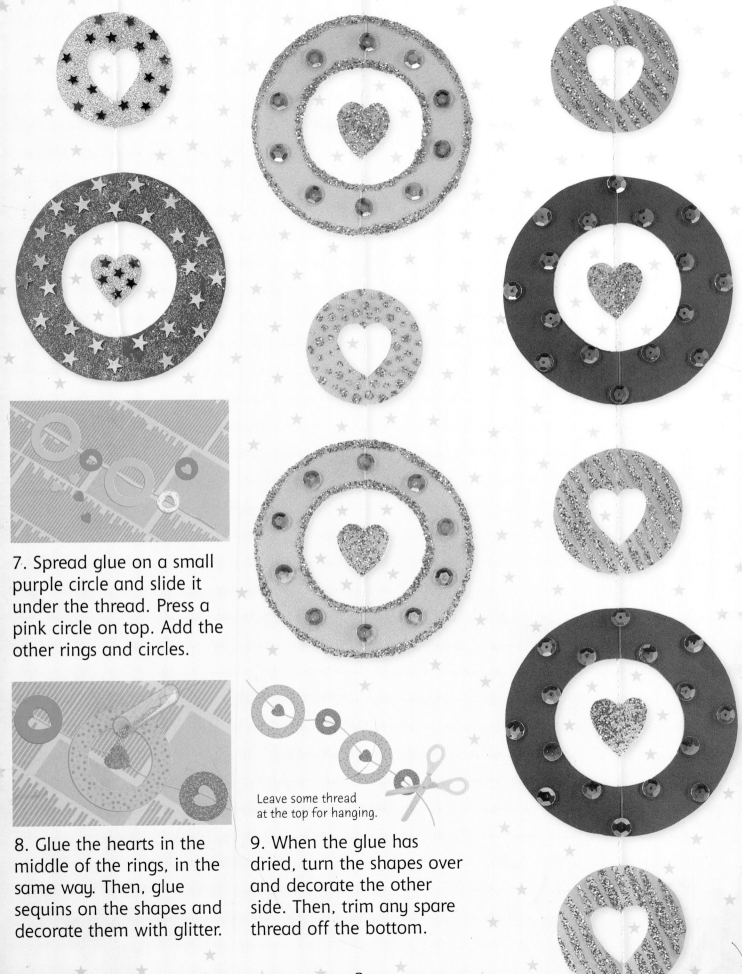

7. Spread glue on a small purple circle and slide it under the thread. Press a pink circle on top. Add the other rings and circles.

8. Glue the hearts in the middle of the rings, in the same way. Then, glue sequins on the shapes and decorate them with glitter.

9. When the glue has dried, turn the shapes over and decorate the other side. Then, trim any spare thread off the bottom.

Leave some thread at the top for hanging.

Flower fairy tiara

The ends of this tiara were taped together to make a crown.

Lay the foil shiny side down.

Press down hard as you roll, to make the band smooth.

1. For the bottom band of the tiara, cut a wide strip of kitchen foil, a little longer than a pipe cleaner. Lay the pipe cleaner on the foil.

2. Squeeze the foil around the pipe cleaner. Roll it into a thin band between your thumb and fingers, then roll it on a flat surface.

3. Cut five thin strips of foil that are half the length of the band. Squeeze them into sticks and roll them on a flat surface.

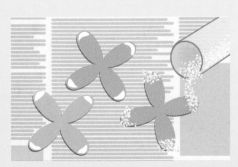

4. Cut out three flowers with four petals each. Dab household glue (PVA) on the tips and sprinkle glitter on. Tap off any excess glitter.

5. Cut out three slightly larger flowers. Dab blobs of glue in the middle of them and press the glittery flowers on top, like this.

6. Curl one end of each foil stick into a spiral. Dab glue in the middle of the flowers and press a foil stick onto each one.

Gently bend the sticks to make them wiggly.

7. When the glue is dry, lay the flowers in a row, glittery side down. Lay the bottom band part of the way up the stems, like this.

8. To attach the flowers to the band of the tiara, bend the bottom of the sticks up. Then, twist them securely around the band.

9. Twist the last two foil sticks onto the band between the flowers. Glue sequins onto the band and gently bend it into a curve.

Try making leaves to go on your tiara, too.

Glittery winged unicorns

1. Dip your finger in white paint and fingerpaint around and around for a body. Fingerpaint a head and a line for the neck.

2. For the legs, cut a strip of cardboard. Then, dip one of the long sides in the paint and drag it across the paper three times.

3. For a bent leg, dip a smaller piece of cardboard in the paint and drag two lines. Use a corner of the cardboard to paint the ears.

Try painting the unicorns in lots of different positions.

These unicorns had glitter lightly sprinkled over them while the paint was still wet.

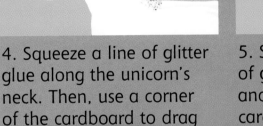

4. Squeeze a line of glitter glue along the unicorn's neck. Then, use a corner of the cardboard to drag curved lines for the mane.

5. Squeeze more lines of glitter glue for the tail and drag them with the cardboard to make them wispy. Then, add a horn.

6. When the glitter glue has dried, use a black felt-tip pen to draw the unicorn's eye, nostril and mouth.

Dip the tape in the glitter so that one end stays sticky.

7. For the sparkly wings, sprinkle some glitter onto a plate. Cut two pieces of sticky tape and dip each one in the glitter.

8. Press the sticky ends of the tape onto the unicorn's back. Fold up the glittery parts, then cut the corners off so they look like wings.

Frosted flowers

1. Fold a piece of tissue paper in half. Place a mug on top and draw around it. Then, keeping the paper folded, cut out the circle.

2. Lay both circles of tissue paper on some newspaper. Then, dab household glue (PVA) around their edges and sprinkle glitter on top.

3. When the glue is dry, gently push one end of a sparkly pipe cleaner through the middle of both circles to make a stem.

Make lots of flowers, then twist the stems together to make one plant.

4. Slide the circles a little way down the stem. Then, firmly pinch the tissue paper and twist it around the stem.

5. Wrap a small piece of sticky tape around the tissue paper and stem, to secure them. Push the petals open a little, if you need to.

6. To make a leaf, fold another piece of tissue paper in half. Draw a leaf shape, then cut it out, keeping the paper folded.

You could use different shades of tissue paper for the flowers.

7. Cut another pipe cleaner in half. Spread glue over one of the leaves, then press one end of the pipe cleaner onto the glue.

8. While the glue is still wet, gently press the other leaf on top. Then, spread glue over the leaf and sprinkle it with glitter.

9. When the glue is dry, lay the stem of the leaf next to the flower stem. Tightly twist them together, then bend the leaf out.

Shimmery bead chains

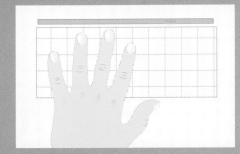

1. Cut a strip of book covering film as long as a thick drinking straw. Make it a little taller than your middle finger.

2. Peel the back off the book film and lay it sticky side up on a newspaper. Then, press the straw along one edge of the film.

Leave the top half of the book film clear.

3. Hold some tinsel over the book film. Then, snip along the tinsel, so that sparkly pieces fall onto the bottom half of the film.

Roll the straw to the top of the film.

4. Cut a strip of tissue paper, then lay it over the pieces of tinsel. Tightly roll the straw over the paper and book film.

You could make long chains from lots of different beads and use them to decorate your room.

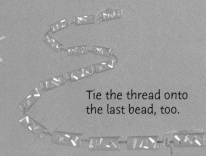

Tie the thread onto the last bead, too.

5. Cut the straw into bead-sized pieces. Tie one bead onto a long piece of thread and string on the rest of the beads to make a chain.

You can use glitter instead of tinsel.

More ideas

Lay the foil shiny side down.

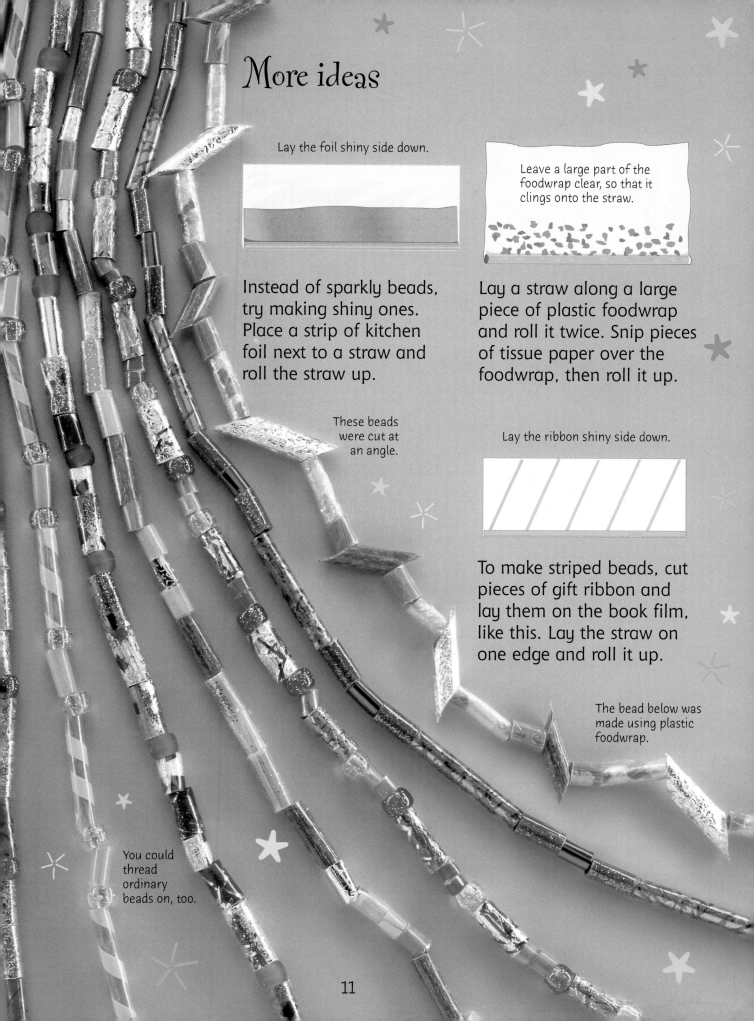

Instead of sparkly beads, try making shiny ones. Place a strip of kitchen foil next to a straw and roll the straw up.

These beads were cut at an angle.

Leave a large part of the foodwrap clear, so that it clings onto the straw.

Lay a straw along a large piece of plastic foodwrap and roll it twice. Snip pieces of tissue paper over the foodwrap, then roll it up.

Lay the ribbon shiny side down.

To make striped beads, cut pieces of gift ribbon and lay them on the book film, like this. Lay the straw on one edge and roll it up.

The bead below was made using plastic foodwrap.

You could thread ordinary beads on, too.

11

Spangly butterflies

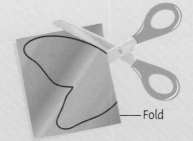

— Fold

You don't need this piece.

1. Cut a piece of shiny wrapping paper and fold it in half. Draw a single butterfly wing against the fold and cut it out.

2. Draw a smaller wing inside the first one, like this. Cut along the line you have drawn, then unfold the wings.

Put the wings shiny side down.

3. Cut a piece of book covering film and peel off the backing. Lay it with the sticky side up and press the wings onto it.

4. Press some sequins onto the book film inside the wings. Then, gently sprinkle a little glitter around the sequins.

Find out on pages 10–11 how to make a sparkly body for your butterfly.

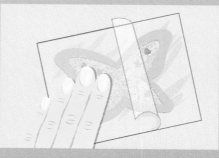

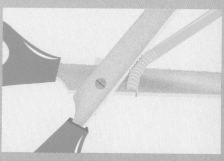

5. Cut another piece of book film and press it over the top of the wings. Smooth it flat, then cut around the wings.

6. For a body, cut the short end off a drinking straw, above the bumpy part. Then, cut into the bumpy part to make the feelers.

12

Decorate the ribbon by gluing on shiny hearts and sequins.

7. Bend the feelers out a little. Then, lay the straw in the middle of the wings and snip the end off, below the wings.

To make a chain of butterflies, thread a butterfly onto the bottom of a long ribbon. Then, knot the ribbon further up and thread on another butterfly.

Make sure the bead is wider than the straw.

8. Make a big knot in the end of a piece of ribbon and thread on a big bead. Then, thread on the straw, with the feelers at the top.

9. Spread glue down the middle of the wings and press on the body. Let the glue dry before hanging the butterfly.

Sparkling boxes

1. Mix some household glue (PVA) with a little water. Then, cut some bright tissue paper into lots of small pieces.

2. Brush the glue over a box and its lid. Then, while the glue is wet, press pieces of tissue paper all over the box, making them overlap.

Try brushing different shapes, such as stars, onto the lids.

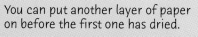

3. Brush on another layer of glue and press on more tissue paper. Add a few more layers, then leave the glue to dry.

4. To make shiny paper sequins, punch lots of holes in a piece of shiny paper. Then, empty the hole puncher onto a plate.

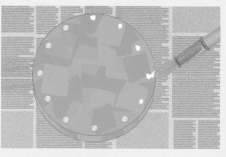

5. With the tip of a small paintbrush, dab little blobs of glue around the edge of the lid. Then, press the sequins onto the glue.

6. Brush a spiral of glue on the lid. Then, sprinkle glitter over the glue and shake off any excess. Let the glue dry.

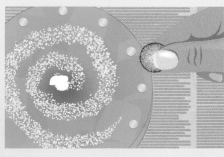

7. To make a sparkly gem, dip a piece of tissue paper in the glue and roll it into a ball. Then, roll the ball in some glitter.

8. Leave the sparkly gem to dry. Then, dab a blob of glue in the middle of the spiral and press the gem onto the glue.

Mermaid bookmark

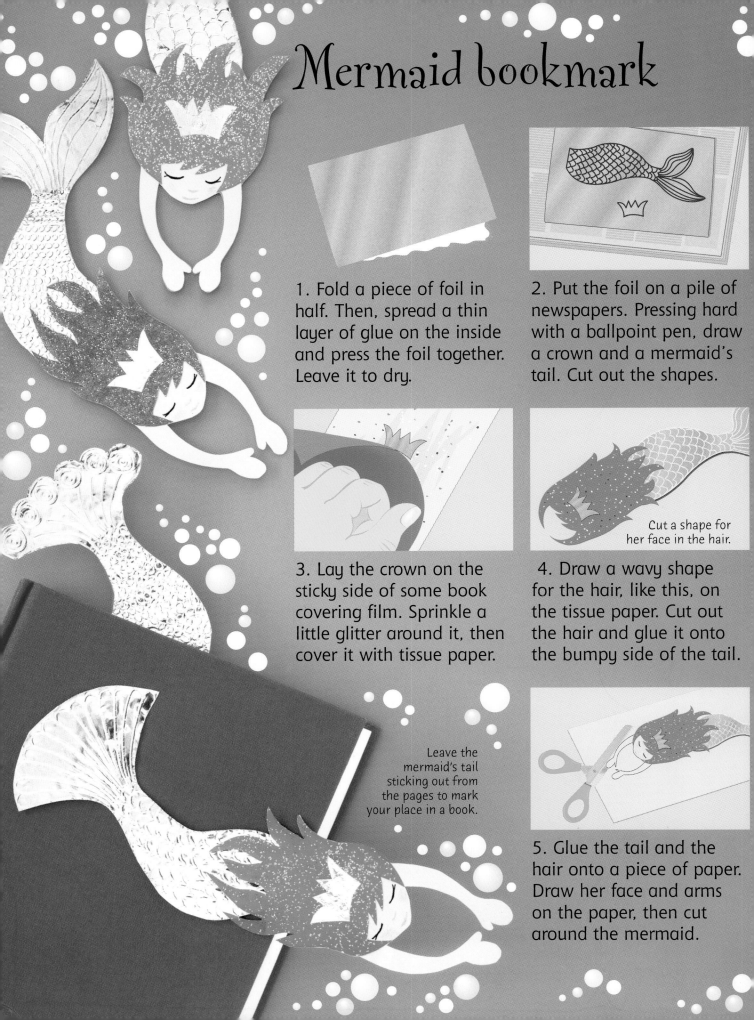

1. Fold a piece of foil in half. Then, spread a thin layer of glue on the inside and press the foil together. Leave it to dry.

2. Put the foil on a pile of newspapers. Pressing hard with a ballpoint pen, draw a crown and a mermaid's tail. Cut out the shapes.

3. Lay the crown on the sticky side of some book covering film. Sprinkle a little glitter around it, then cover it with tissue paper.

Cut a shape for her face in the hair.

4. Draw a wavy shape for the hair, like this, on the tissue paper. Cut out the hair and glue it onto the bumpy side of the tail.

Leave the mermaid's tail sticking out from the pages to mark your place in a book.

5. Glue the tail and the hair onto a piece of paper. Draw her face and arms on the paper, then cut around the mermaid.

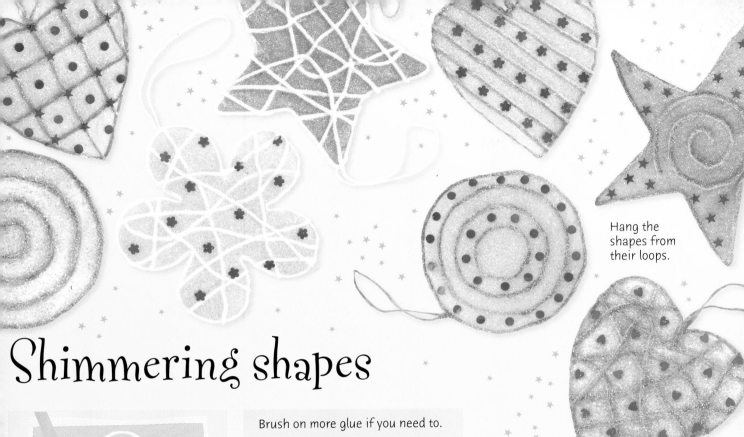

Hang the shapes from their loops.

Shimmering shapes

1. Draw a heart on a piece of tissue paper and lay it on some plastic foodwrap. Brush household glue (PVA) over the pencil line.

Brush on more glue if you need to.

2. Press a length of thread onto the glue. At the top of the heart, make a loop with the thread and press the end into the glue.

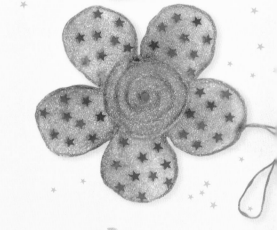

Don't worry if the ends go over the edge.

3. Brush a thin layer of glue inside the heart. Then, cut pieces of thread and press them into the glue, so that they overlap.

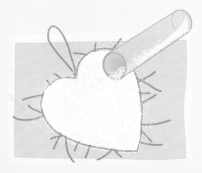

4. Brush another layer of glue over the top. Lightly sprinkle glitter over the shape and leave it until the glue has completely dried.

5. Peel the tissue paper off the foodwrap and cut around the heart. Then, glue sequins between the threads to decorate it.

17

Glitter bugs

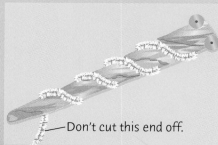

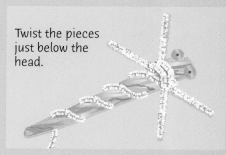
Twist the pieces just below the head.

—Don't cut this end off.

1. Cut a square of foil as wide as your hand span and roll it into a sausage. Press one end flat and glue sequins on for eyes.

2. Wind a pipe cleaner along the length of the body from just below the eyes. Leave any extra as you will need it later.

3. For the wings, cut a pipe cleaner in half. Twist one half around the body. Twist on the other half too, then bend the ends out, like this.

Use two different shades of paper.

4. To print the wings, place a leaf, with the veins facing up, on some newspaper. Lightly brush over the leaf with silver or gold paint.

Most of these bugs were made with shiny craft foil.

5. Press the painted side of the leaf onto some tissue paper to print four leaves. Cut them out when the paint is dry.

6. Lay the wings painted side down. Put the bug on top, upside down, like this. Bend the pipe cleaners so that they lie on the wings.

You could use the bugs to decorate plant pots by pushing the stick into the soil.

7. Tape the pipe cleaners onto the wings. You can then spread open the wings by bending the pipe cleaners.

The foil should be long enough to cover the stick.

8. Cut a strip of foil. Tape one end to the blunt end of a satay or kebab stick. Wind the foil along the stick, then tape the end.

9. Place the blunt end of the stick along the extra length of pipe cleaner. Wind the pipe cleaner tightly around the stick.

Flying fairy card

1. Cut two rectangles of paper the same size, one blue and one green. Fold the green rectangle in half so the short edges meet.

Make sure both cuts are the same length.

2. Make two small cuts in the middle of the folded edge, to make a flap. Crease the flap to the front, then to the back.

3. Open the card and push the flap through the card, like this. Close the card and smooth it flat, then open it again.

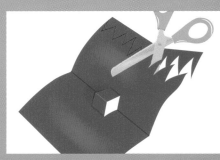

4. For the grass, draw a zigzag line across the card, above the flap. Then, cut along the line you have drawn, like this.

Decorate the flowers with glitter and sequins to make them more sparkly.

Don't glue the flap.

5. For the sky, fold the blue paper in half. Then, glue the green card onto it, making sure that the middle folds line up.

20

Shake off any excess glitter.

6. For the fairy, cut out some wings and spread household glue (PVA) over them. Sprinkle them with glitter and let them dry.

7. For the fairy's head, cut a circle from pink paper. Cut out a shape for her hair, then glue it onto the head. Draw a face.

To make your card even more sparkly, add a glittery sun and clouds.

8. Cut out shapes for her dress, arms and feet. Glue the arms and feet onto the back of the dress and glue the head onto the front.

9. Dab glue on the wings and press them onto the back of her dress. Then, decorate the fairy with sequins and glitter glue.

10. Glue the fairy onto the top of the flap. Then, decorate the card by cutting out flowers and gluing them onto the grass.

Ice castle collage

Glue the mountains along the bottom edge of the paper.

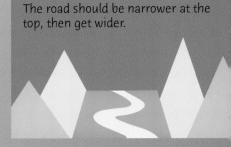

The road should be narrower at the top, then get wider.

1. For the mountains, cut different shades of pink paper into different sizes of triangles. Make one bigger than all the others.

2. Cut the tip off the biggest triangle. Glue the other mountains onto a large piece of blue paper. Glue the big one on last.

3. On a piece of pale pink paper, draw a wiggly road to go on the big mountain. Cut out the shape you have drawn and glue it on.

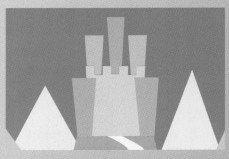

Draw small windows in silver felt-tip pen.

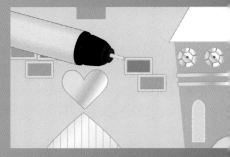

4. Cut out three very tall towers and glue them on. Cut out a wall and glue it on. Then, cut out and glue on two short towers.

5. Cut out triangles from shiny paper for the roofs and glue them on. Cut out and glue on a door and windows, too.

6. Decorate the castle with sequins and shiny shapes. Draw bricks, and outline the bricks and the windows with a silver felt-tip pen.

7. Pour some granulated sugar and a little glitter into a container. Then, shake the container so that they mix together.

8. Dab household glue (PVA) onto the road, the mountains and the roofs. Pour the sugar mixture on, then tap off any excess.

Cut out a foil shape
for the moon and decorate
the sky with star stickers.

Sparkly picture frame

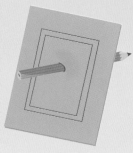

1. Lay the picture you want to frame on a piece of thick paper. Then, use a pencil to draw lightly around the picture.

2. Draw another rectangle inside your pencil lines. Then, push a sharp pencil into the middle of this rectangle to make a hole.

These frames were decorated using ideas from the page opposite.

3. Push one scissor blade into the hole. Then, cut around the edge of the small rectangle to make a 'window' in the frame.

4. Cut strips of paper that are as wide as the frame. Then, cut the strips into squares and glue them around the frame, like this.

5. Make your picture frame sparkly by using stickers or gluing on sequins. You could use glitter and glitter glue to decorate it as well.

6. Lay the frame on top of your picture. Turn them over and tape the picture in place. Tape on a loop of thread for hanging.

Decorating ideas

Use glitter glue to draw around the squares on the frame. When the glitter glue has dried, glue lots of sequins inside each square.

To make sparkly spots, dip the tip of a paintbrush in household glue (PVA). Dab blobs of glue on the frame and sprinkle glitter on top.

Glue lots of pieces of gift ribbon along the sides of the frame. Then, cut off any ends that overlap the frame.

See pages 6-7 for how to make a unicorn picture.

Follow the steps on pages 20-21 to make a fairy like this one.

Twinkling twirlers

1. Place a small plate on a piece of thick, yellow paper. Draw around it and cut it out. Then, do the same with pink paper.

2. Glue the two circles together. When the glue is dry, draw a spiral from the edge into the middle and cut along it.

Keep the paper folded as you cut.

3. Fold a piece of thick, yellow paper in half. Draw five stars and cut them out. Then, cut stars from a piece of pink paper, too.

4. Lay the stars on some newspaper and brush household glue (PVA) over them. Sprinkle them with glitter and let them dry.

The twirlers will sparkle more if you hang them in a place where they can spin and catch the light.

5. Cut ten pieces of gold and pink gift ribbon. Cut the pieces so that they are roughly the length of your hand.

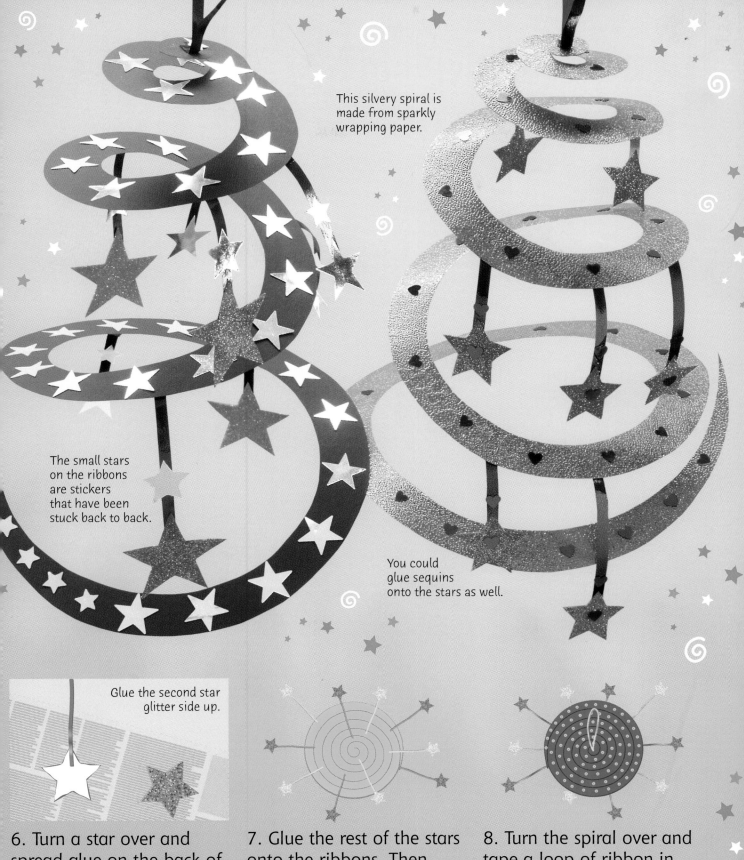

This silvery spiral is made from sparkly wrapping paper.

The small stars on the ribbons are stickers that have been stuck back to back.

You could glue sequins onto the stars as well.

Glue the second star glitter side up.

6. Turn a star over and spread glue on the back of it. Press a piece of gift ribbon onto the glue and press another star on top.

7. Glue the rest of the stars onto the ribbons. Then, glue the ends of the ribbons onto the spiral, with their shiny side down.

8. Turn the spiral over and tape a loop of ribbon in the middle. Then, decorate both sides of the spiral using sequins or stickers.

Decorated elephants

These chains of elephants were arranged in a curve before being taped together.

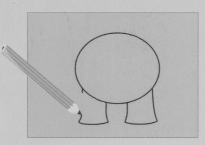

1. On a piece of thick paper, in pencil, lightly draw an oval for an elephant's body. Draw shapes for the legs as well.

Erase the pencil lines later.

2. Draw a thick trunk with a circle at the end. For the tail, draw a thin triangle with a tassel at the end, that looks like this.

The elephants should all face the same way.

3. Cut out the elephant. Draw around it on different papers, then cut out the elephants. Draw eyes and ears in black felt-tip pen.

The patterns on this elephant's body were drawn with a gold pen.

4. Cut out shapes for the elephants' tusks and toenails from shiny paper or foil. Then, glue them onto each elephant.

Use a small piece of tape so that you can't see it from the front.

5. Decorate the elephants by cutting out paper shapes and gluing them on. Use sequins or beads, pens and glitter glue, too.

6. Make a small cut in one elephant's trunk, like this. Then, slot the thin part of another elephant's tail into the slit.

7. Slot all the elephants together, then carefully turn the chain over. Secure the tails to the trunks with small pieces of sticky tape.

Dazzling party masks

Leave gaps between the strips, so that there are white patches.

1. Cut a piece of pink and a piece of blue tissue paper into long strips. The strips should be the width of two of your fingers.

2. Glue the blue strips diagonally across a piece of cardboard, leaving gaps between them. Then, glue the pink strips over them.

3. When the glue is dry, turn the cardboard over. Lay a pair of sunglasses on the cardboard, like this, and draw around them.

Use the outline of the sunglasses as a guide for the eyeholes.

4. Draw shapes where your eyes will be. Then, draw a mask around the outline of the glasses. Cut out the mask you have drawn.

5. Press the point of a sharp pencil through the eyeholes. Push one scissor blade into the holes. Then, cut out both eyeholes.

6. Turn the mask over. Draw lines of glitter glue along all the edges of the tissue paper strips. Let the glitter glue dry.

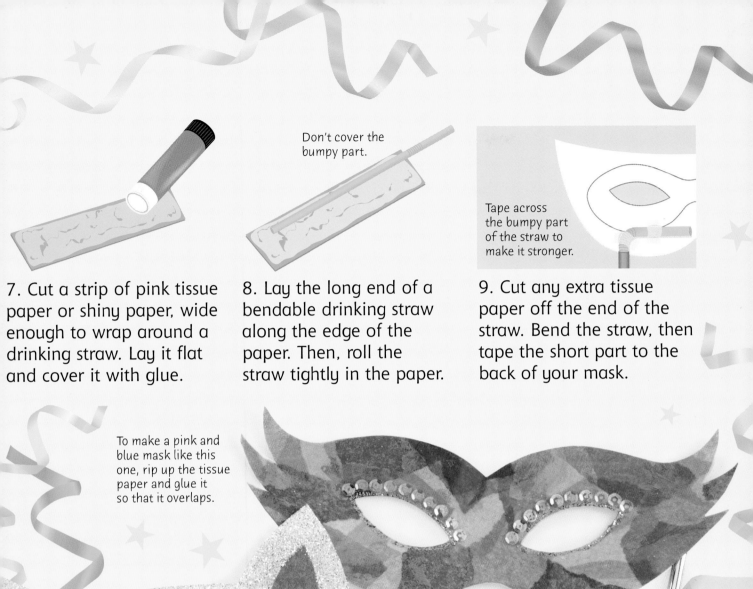

Don't cover the bumpy part.

Tape across the bumpy part of the straw to make it stronger.

7. Cut a strip of pink tissue paper or shiny paper, wide enough to wrap around a drinking straw. Lay it flat and cover it with glue.

8. Lay the long end of a bendable drinking straw along the edge of the paper. Then, roll the straw tightly in the paper.

9. Cut any extra tissue paper off the end of the straw. Bend the straw, then tape the short part to the back of your mask.

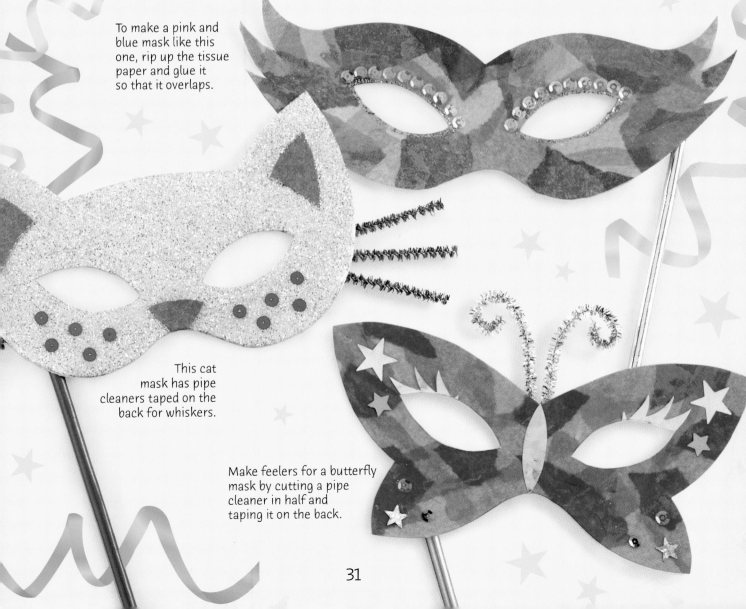

To make a pink and blue mask like this one, rip up the tissue paper and glue it so that it overlaps.

This cat mask has pipe cleaners taped on the back for whiskers.

Make feelers for a butterfly mask by cutting a pipe cleaner in half and taping it on the back.

Gift tag ideas

You can make lots of different gift tags using the techniques in this book. Here are some of the ideas you could try:

Make a circular tag with a ring and a heart from pages 2–3.

Make a glitter bug as on pages 18–19. Glue the wings onto the gift tag, then press the foil body on top.

This fairy was made using the same method as the flying fairy on pages 20–21.

Try making a mini ice castle (see pages 22–23).

The tag above was made using picture frame ideas from pages 24–25.

Cut out flower shapes like those on the flying fairy card on pages 20–21.

Turn a glitter bug (pages 18–19) into a butterfly by gluing on foil feelers before gluing the body on top.

Photographic manipulation: Emma Julings, Mike Wheatley and John Russell
First published in 2004 by Usborne Publishing Ltd., 83-85 Saffron Hill, London, EC1N 8RT www.usborne.com